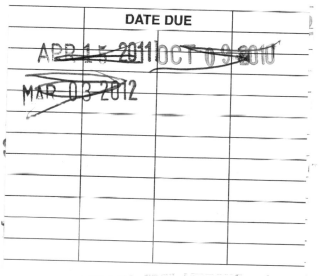

DATE DUE

APR 1 5 2011	OCT 0 9 2010	
MAR 03 2012		

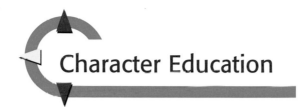

Character Education

Self-Respect

by Lucia Raatma

Consultant:
Madonna Murphy, Ph.D.
Professor of Education
University of St. Francis, Joliet, Illinois
Author, *Character Education in America's
Blue Ribbon Schools*

Bridgestone Books
an imprint of Capstone Press
Mankato, Minnesota

Bridgestone Books are published by Capstone Press
151 Good Counsel Drive, P.O. Box 669, Mankato, Minnesota 56002
http://www.capstone-press.com

Library of Congress Cataloging-in-Publication Data
Raatma, Lucia.
    Self-respect/by Lucia Raatma.
    p. cm.—(Character education)
    Includes bibliographical references and index.
    ISBN 0-7368-1133-8
    1. Self-esteem in children—Juvenile literature. [1. Self-esteem.] I. Title. II. Series.
BF723.S3 R32 2002
155.4'182—dc21   2001003433

Summary: Explains the virtue of self-respect and gives tips on how to have self-respect in
    your home, school, and community.

Editorial Credits
Sarah Lynn Schuette, editor; Karen Risch, product planning editor; Jennifer Schonborn, cover
    production designer and illustrator; Alta Schaffer, photo researcher

Photo Credits
Archive Photos, 18
Capstone Press/Gary Sundermeyer, cover, 4, 6, 12, 14, 16, 20
Comstock, Inc., 10
Photo Network/Myrleen Ferguson, 8

1 2 3 4 5 6 07 06 05 04 03 02

Table of Contents

Self-Respect

Self-respect means believing in your worth as a person. It means trying to be the best person you can be. Respecting yourself feels good. It means taking care of your body and mind. People with self-respect set goals for themselves.

goal
something that you aim
for or work toward

Having Self-Respect

Having self-respect means being proud of who you are. It means being proud of your accomplishments. Having self-respect also means honoring your own thoughts and feelings. You can feel good about yourself when you have self-respect.

accomplishment
a task or a job someone
has done well

Self-Respect at Home

Respecting your home shows that you respect yourself. You can set a goal to put your clean clothes away. Try to meet your goal every week. Showing self-respect at home means that you are an important member of your family.

Self-Respect with Your Friends

You and your friends may have a lot in common. People who have self-respect do not use peer pressure on their friends. They do not force others to do things they do not want to do. You can choose friends who will support and respect you.

support
to help, encourage, and believe in someone

Setting a Good Example

You show self-respect when you set a good example for others. People who respect themselves think carefully about the choices they make. You can set a good example for your family by wearing your seatbelt.

This is my very best work.

Self-Respect at School

You can be proud of being a good student. Finishing your assignments is important. You may need to finish an art project. Set a goal to finish the project before you go outside for recess. Meeting your goals at school shows self-respect.

assignment
a job that is given to someone

Self-Respect in Your Community

People who respect themselves work
hard to be trustworthy and honest.
They pay for things in stores. They
do not lie or steal. You can show
self-respect by being kind to people
in your community.

"I'm not concerned with your liking or disliking me...all I ask is that you respect me as a human being."
—Jackie Robinson

Jackie Robinson

Jackie Robinson joined the Brooklyn Dodgers in 1947. He became the first African American to play major league baseball. Some people thought Jackie should not play. But Jackie respected himself. He was proud of his baseball skills.

major league baseball
a group of baseball teams; players in this league get paid to play baseball.

Building Self-Respect

One way to build self-respect is by respecting your body. Work hard to keep your body clean and healthy. You can also build self-respect by showing respect to others. Make eye contact and smile when you speak to them.

Hands On: Make a Scrapbook

People who have self-respect are proud of their accomplishments. You can make a scrapbook of your accomplishments.

What You Need

10 pieces of colored paper   Ribbons, certificates, or pictures
Stapler   Glue
Markers

What You Do

1. Put the pieces of paper into a stack.
2. Staple along the left edge of the stack. Make sure the staples go through each piece of paper. This will be your scrapbook.
3. Write your name on the cover and decorate it with the markers.
4. Gather ribbons, certificates, or pictures of things that you have accomplished. Ask an adult if it is okay to use these items in your scrapbook.
5. Think about your actions and other ways you show self-respect.
6. Open the scrapbook and glue or draw the items on different pages of your scrapbook.
7. Use markers to write why you are proud of each item.
8. Add new items to the scrapbook when you accomplish new things.

Words to Know

accomplishment (uh-KOM-plish-muhnt)—a task or a job someone has done well; people can be proud of their accomplishments.

assignment (uh-SINE-muhnt)—a job that is given to someone; teachers give assignments such as art projects at school.

goal (GOHL)—something that you aim for or work toward; people who have self-respect set positive goals for themselves.

respect (ri-SPEKT)—a belief in the qualities and worth of others and yourself

worth (WURTH)—the quality that makes someone or something important

Read More

Kent, Susan. *Learning How to Feel Good about Yourself.* The Violence Prevention Library. New York: PowerKids Press, 2001.
Raatma, Lucia. *Jackie Robinson.* Compass Point Early Biographies. Minneapolis: Compass Point Books, 2001.

Internet Sites

A Person of Character
http://www.cortland.edu/www/c4n5rs/char_v.htm
The Story on Self-Esteem
http://kidshealth.org/kid/feeling/emotion/self_esteem.html

Index